"A simple, straight-forward invitation to go beyond using meditation as a tool and instead dwell in meditation until it pours from your skin and scents your breath—becoming the foundation by which you take action in everyday life. A lovely offering to the world."

—**Zenju Earthlyn Manuel**, Zen priest and author of *The Deepest Peace* and *The Way of Tenderness*

"In today's buddhaverse, Claude AnShin Thomas is one of the most influential and beloved teachers. Here he distills and shares with generosity, love, and clarity the wisdom he has earned through the practice of meditation and a remarkable life devoted to the dharma, peacemaking, and serving others. This is a book, and a rare teacher, worthy of our trust."

—**Charles Johnson**, winner of the National Book Award and author of *Turning the Wheel: Essays on Buddhism and Writing*

"This book is imbued with wisdom and compassion born of AnShin's personal experiences as a combat veteran in the Vietnam War, his soul searching and introspection that has characterized his journey of healing, and his many years of experience as a Zen Buddhist monk leading meditation retreats. Wise and wonderful, comprehensible and readable, I highly recommend it."

—**Camillo Mac Bica**, PhD, author of *Beyond PTSD: The Moral Casualties of War*

BRINGING MEDITATION TO LIFE

108 TEACHINGS ON THE PATH OF ZEN PRACTICE

CLAUDE ANSHIN THOMAS

OAKWOOD PUBLISHING

Mary Esther, Florida

2021

Oakwood Publishing, a division of
Zaltho Foundation, Inc.
548 Mary Esther Cutoff NW, PMB 319
Fort Walton Beach, FL 32548
www.zaltho.org

Cover design by Hilary Moreno
Interior design by Jazmin Welch, Fleck Creative Studio

Library of Congress Control Number:
2020924393

ISBN hardcover 978-1-7362934-3-0
ISBN paperback 978-1-7362934-0-9
ISBN ebook 978-1-7362934-1-6
ISBN audiobook 978-1-7362934-2-3

Contents

Introduction

have had the privilege of teaching meditation practice since I was ordained as a Zen Buddhist monk in 1994. Since then I have traveled across the United States and around the world offering the instructions that I received from my teachers and sharing the essential message that meditation and daily life are not two separate things.

Our practice starts with—and is continually supported by—engaging in formal sitting meditation on a daily basis. However, our practice doesn't stop there. We can bring meditation and breath awareness into everything that we do throughout the day. When we do this, our practice and our lives will flourish.

When I give talks, I reserve a portion of the time for questions and responses. I don't call this exchange "questions and answers," because, as I always say to those in attendance, I don't have any answers. I can only respond to their questions based on my own life experience, sharing my perspective on what it means to live a life fully committed to a disciplined spiritual practice and rooted in self-reflection.

The short texts that make up the chapters of this book are drawn mainly from these question-and-response sessions. A few of the chapters consist of short passages from my memoir, *At Hell's Gate: A Soldier's Journey from War to Peace*. I have also included in this book some of my favorite quotations from Zen literature.

Establishing a Daily Meditation Practice

The foundation of Zen practice is sitting meditation, or *zazen*. I encourage you to make meditation part of your daily routine. When you get up in the morning, before you do anything else, sit for at least five minutes, whether you want to or not.

It's helpful, though not required, to create a small, simple altar as follows: place an incense holder in the center, between a flower to the left and a candle to the right. Before you sit, light the candle and some incense.

You can sit on a chair, a meditation cushion, or on the edge of your bed. When sitting make sure that you are sitting in a solid, stable position. There should be three points of contact. If you're seated on a mediation cushion or a meditation bench, the three points of contact will be your bottom and your knees. If you're sitting in a chair or on the edge of your bed, the three points are your bottom and your feet.

Notice your body in space. Make sure that your ears are aligned with your shoulders, that your nose is aligned with your navel, and that your back is straight with your hips pressed slightly forward.

From this upright posture, connect with your breath, breathing in through your nose and out through your mouth. As you breathe, pay attention to the precise point at which the breath enters the body and then exits the body. Anchor your attention at those points.

When you breathe in, be conscious that you do not cut the breath off at the diaphragm. You will know that this is happening if your chest expands and your shoulders rise. When you breathe in, breathe into your abdomen. (You will know that this is happening because your stomach will expand when you breathe in and will contract when you breathe out.) Don't mentally follow your breath all the way through your body. Keep your attention anchored at the points of entry and exit from the body. But do breathe deeply into the abdomen.

Sit each day, for at least five minutes every morning and every evening. Sitting consistently each day is more supportive and sustainable than sitting sporadically for longer periods of time. We always have five minutes. If we tell ourselves that only longer periods of time count, our minds will also eventually tell us that we don't have the time, that we can put it off until another day. Now is the time. Sit for five minutes, first thing, every morning and again just before going to bed at night.

It's a simple practice, really, but how quickly we build resistance to following this program. But imagine you felt unwell for a prolonged period of time, so you decided to consult a doctor. After the examination and some tests, the doctor tells you that you have slow-growing cancer, a rare form that could be treated by following a simple regimen every day: in the morning when you wake up, light a candle, offer some incense, and sit still for five minutes. Then before you go to bed, repeat the process. Doing this will arrest your illness. Do you think that you would hesitate to do this every day? This is what I am offering you, a treatment that can heal the illness of suffering.

However, this healing does not mean that our pain, discomfort, and uneasiness go away and never come back. It simply means that we have the possibility to develop a more conscious and honest relationship with our suffering so that when it visits us, in all of the many ways that it can, we are not controlled by it. This is the path of practice, of healing and transformation.

1

Meditation is a Way of Living

Meditation is not just something we do while seated on a cushion or in a meditation hall, it's a way of living. The practice of meditation can be present and support us in all things, in every moment, like a life jacket that keeps us from drowning. Without it, we will sink into the sea of *samsara*, the sea of our confusion and suffering.

By living a life rooted in meditation, we have the opportunity to recognize our repeating patterns of suffering and begin to establish a more conscious relationship with these patterns so that they no longer control us. Through this process, through living a life rooted in a disciplined, committed meditation practice, we have the opportunity to finally experience the wonder of being alive.

2

The Mind Is Always Generating Thoughts

Many people think that meditation is about stopping our thoughts or having a blank mind, but this is simply not possible. Our mind is of the nature to generate thoughts. Meditation is about learning not to get swept away by our thoughts.

Initially, the technique of counting our breaths from one to ten, then back again, can be helpful. Count "one" for the first cycle of breath (the first in-breath and out-breath), then "two" for the next cycle, and so on. When you notice that your mind has wandered off, simply begin counting again from one.

The point of this technique is not to master getting to ten and then back to one, nor do we count this way to block out our thoughts. Counting this way simply helps us to notice when we get swept away by our thoughts and lose contact with our breath. This will happen, sometimes very quickly. When it does, we just return our attention to our breath and count "one."

Meditation gives us the opportunity to develop a new kind of relationship to our thinking. We learn to be the observer of our thoughts, without attaching to them or rejecting them. We start to notice that thoughts and feelings are not so solid, real, or lasting: they arise, they have a certain life cycle, and then they pass away. If I am concentrated on my breath, then all things are present. My thoughts are here, my feelings are here. I am just not drawn as deeply into them, and I am not controlled by them.

3

Living Peacefully with Unpeacefulness

One of the mistakes people often make when they take up the practice of mindfulness is that they form a false image of it. They think that being mindful means not being afraid, that it means being calm and at peace at all times. This is not living in mindfulness. Mindfulness and mental calm are related, but they are not the same. For me, living in mindfulness means that I can live peacefully in non-peace, that I can accept the reality of non-calm.

In all our lives, there are moments of calm and moments of non-calm. If I live in mindfulness, I can accept that these moments come and go—like a gentle rain or like a hurricane, but they do come and go. In mindfulness I see their beauty when they are here, I can celebrate what they offer me, knowing that they will pass and also knowing that they may return. If I am living in mindfulness, if I can look deeply into the nature of myself and touch my suffering, I can learn to live with my fear, my doubts, my insecurity, my confusion, my anger. My task is to dwell in these places like still water.

4

The Illusion of a Separate Self

One of the foundational teachings of Buddhism is that in truth there is no separate self. Yes, my individual physical being exists, but my existence did not come out of nothing. My existence depends on my parents, grandparents, great grandparents—all the previous generations. All these people are present in me. They live within my physical, emotional, and spiritual DNA. In what sense am I separate from them?

It's also worthwhile contemplating our dependence on the natural world. For example, if bees ceased to exist and pollinate our crops, humanity would struggle to produce the food we need to survive. My life is dependent on bees, on plants, and on many other life forms. From this perspective, the idea of a separate, independent self is a myth. My intellect can create the illusion of a self, but this is just a construction of the mind. Through consistent meditation practice, we will begin to recognize the separate self as a fiction, and we will begin to experience our interconnection with all life more directly and intimately.

5

On Silence

During meditation retreats, we are mostly silent. Silence is a valuable practice, and it is about so much more than not talking. Silence is about working with the activity of the mind, all the thinking about this and that, the constant craving of the mind to escape from what is. In silence, we often have a greater chance of seeing how our mind and emotions operate and to discover the wisdom that connects all things.

People often don't like silence because in silence we are left with ourselves. There is no escape from our thoughts, feelings, and perceptions. If we are new to meditation practice and haven't spent much time with ourselves, at times the silence can seem nearly unbearable.

I still remember my early days and weeks at the first Buddhist monastery where I trained. I would be walking the grounds, and I would pass by one of the monks. Out of a sense of politeness, of wanting to connect (and out of uneasiness), I would say, "Good morning." The monks would just pass by, saying nothing and acting, from my perspective at the time, as if I didn't exist. My immediate reaction was to feel offended and to assume they didn't like me. As my training continued, my mind went through many changes until finally I got to the point where the silence of the monks to my greetings no longer felt personal or no longer felt like a rejection. In fact, I began to experience the silence as a great relief. I was freed of the social conventions that often left me feeling empty and not seen or heard anyway. In the silence there was a certain comfort in relating to others that I hadn't experienced before.

Practicing silently in a group invites us to experience another kind of consciousness, another kind of awareness, and new ways of connecting with each other. There is a deepening of awareness and a great opportunity to clarify the mind.

6

The Greatest Barrier

"Many have the hope that spiritual training, Zen, will lift them out of the ordinary round of life, that they will in some measure become extraordinary, unique, or that they will experience extraordinary states of mind, perpetual bliss, a non-stop high. Yet it is precisely this wish that is the first and greatest barrier to true practice."

—**Albert Low,** *The Iron Cow of Zen*

7

There Is No Other Place
for Practice

Please understand that you do not need to go somewhere else to find peace and healing. You don't need to go to a monastery or on a retreat, though this can sometimes be helpful. In reality, the monastery or retreat is not outside of you—it is you and your everyday life. In a real way, you are already on retreat right now, as you read these words. Meditation practice and your ordinary daily life are not two separate things. Once you understand this, your life will begin to transform.

8

My Healing and Your Healing
Are Not Separate

I am a combat veteran of the Vietnam War who lives with the lasting wounds that often come with such service. I live with post-traumatic stress, which is a component of moral injury—the deep psychological and spiritual wound caused by having betrayed what is right and having been encouraged to do so by those in positions of power and authority.

One of my Zen teachers said to me, "When you heal, you heal for all veterans of all wars." Back at that time I said to myself, *This guy is out of his mind. What kind of mystical mumbo jumbo is he talking about?* However, I kept practicing meditation—sitting, walking, eating, and working meditation. And one day awareness washed over me like a warm shower, and I knew; I had come to understand what he meant. My healing and the healing of others are not separate.

This new understanding and awareness was not a product of the intellect. Settled in a disciplined practice, one rooted in sitting meditation and just doing the next thing, I became more conscious of the limits of my intellect. My life began to open up, to transform, in ways that I could never have imagined. This was my encouragement to continue. So, I continue to walk just to walk, to sit just to sit, to eat just to eat, to do what is right in front of me to do. I just do this and see what unfolds next. What else will grow out of this commitment to the reality of not-knowing?

9

How Long to Meditate

When we practice sitting meditation, the length of time is not as important as the intention that we bring to the cushion: to learn to be present with everything we do. Yes, sitting practice is the root, the foundation of a disciplined spiritual practice, however just sitting on the cushion is not meditation. We sit so that we can see what prevents us from wholeheartedly engaging in our lives.

Any ideas that we have of what a disciplined spiritual practice is, more often than not, miss the mark. At the root of practice is the instruction to just stop, stay concentrated with the breath, and watch. Pay attention to what turns up. How long we sit is not the point. The point is to start and then to continue regularly, day after day. The point is to allow the practice to take root and grow.

10

Go Deeper Than Enjoyment

Meditation is not about enjoyment. Go deeper than your ideas of enjoyment. Stay with it, stay with the process. Just settle, surrender, let go. Breathe into your abdomen, breathe out. Keep going, and don't give up. Then you will begin to experience the benefit. Meditation brings you right into contact with your resistance. This is important. Resistance and doubt are an important and valuable part of the process. When you experience these so-called obstacles, just continue to sit and see what unfolds.

11

Keeping a Sense of Wonder

The only way that I stand a chance of coming to a place of awakening is to stop thinking that I have already arrived somewhere or that I know anything for certain. I must keep a sense of curiosity and wonder. Through the process of sitting meditation, through concentration on the breath, my relationship to myself and the world can transform. However, for this to happen, I must be willing to let go of my ideas—all of my ideas about how life ought to be. If I let go of my ideas, the reality of how things are begins to show itself. At this juncture of my life my commitment is to continue this process of discovery, to explore how to work with all that is revealed to me, and to strengthen my growing awareness.

12

The Four Essentials of Zen

I n my own practice, study, and teaching over the years, four essential aspects of Zen Buddhist practice have come to stand out to me.

1. Silence—The foundation of Zen practice is a committed, consistent, silent sitting meditation practice supported by an authentic teacher and a practice community. Zen practice is about bringing more silence into our lives and about bringing the silence that is sitting meditation into everything we do. "Silence" in this sense doesn't just mean the absence of noise. Anyone who has sat in meditation understands that the workings of the mind, even in the absence of external sounds, can be deafening. The practice of silence is about noticing and changing our relationship with the internal

and external noises that accompany us day and night, neither rejecting them nor attaching to them.

2. Discipline—An essential ingredient in our practice is the commitment and determination to keep going no matter what, to continue to sit just to sit, to walk to just walk, to eat just to eat, whether we feel like it or not. Along the way, we will encounter doubts and challenges. Our minds will tell us we don't really need to sit today, that it doesn't matter, or that it's not "working." Our discipline is to continue to practice each day—on and off the cushion—and see what unfolds.

3. Ritual—Part of a committed Zen practice is learning the rituals and services that have been handed down from teacher to student for generations. "The object of ceremony," according to the *Sutra of Hui-neng*, "is to curb arrogance." Our lives are full of ritual, not only in the meditation hall but throughout the day. Our practice is to approach everything we do in the zendo with great care and attention and then to carry that into all aspects of our daily lives.

4. Study—Our practice is deepened by reading classical Buddhist texts such as the *Dhammapada*, the *Heart Sutra*, the *Diamond Sutra*, the *Lankavatara Sutra*, and the *Avatamsaka Sutra*. But we must remember that waking up is not an intellectual process. When studying these texts, we read just to read, keeping ever conscious that

the heart of practice does not rest in the words but rather in the space between the words, in the space between the letters.

13

The First Precept:
Do Not Kill

The first Buddhist precept is to abstain from killing. This might sound like an easy precept to follow. "I've never killed," you might say. Is that true? Our houses and furnishings, even the pages of this book, are made from killing trees. If we look more carefully, we will see that our lives are sustained at the expense of other life forms. The question then becomes: How can I live this precept?

One way that has become apparent for me is to not eat any fish, meat, or poultry. With this step, I make a decision to not support the more obvious institutions of killing. Then it's up to me to continue to look deeply at my life, with awareness and honesty, to see how I can reduce or eliminate other forms of killing. It's a never-ending process.

By engaging with the Buddhist precepts, I have come to recognize and respect the law of karma, or cause and effect: for every action there is a consequence. Most people think of karma as "what comes around goes around," but this is too simplistic. We cannot know with certainty what the exact consequence of any action will be. We can only be certain that anger will produce more anger, hatred will generate more hatred, and that killing will lead to more killing—somewhere, sometime, somehow. So, if I want the world to be different, I must put all my effort into a disciplined spiritual practice so that I can be shown, through this practice, how to live differently.

14

Gentle Determination

The process of waking up can seem slow and never ending. At other times it can seem sudden, even startling. If we enter into a disciplined spiritual practice with a fixed idea of what we want to accomplish, or what this accomplishment ought to look and feel like, we will become frustrated when our ideas are not borne out—and certainly when they are not manifesting quickly enough.

In Zen practice, we must develop an unwavering commitment to waking up while at the same time abandoning any ideas or preconceptions about what this awakening will look like or how it will impact us.

On the path of practice, we must also be patient and sensitive with ourselves for the actions that we take in forgetfulness; we must be gentle with ourselves without becoming lazy or making excuses.

15

Falsely Accused

A Zen monk lived alone in a temple on the outskirts of a small village. It came to pass that a young woman from a prosperous family in the village became pregnant out of wedlock, and her parents demanded to know who the father was. To protect her lover, the young woman said that the Zen monk was the child's father, and the actual father left town.

The villagers went to confront the monk, who, when faced with this scandalous and false accusation, did not attempt to defend himself. He listened quietly, and, once he understood the situation, offered to care for the child. Once the child was born, he raised it as if it were his own.

Several years later, the young woman's lover returned to the village. After the couple reunited, they told everyone the truth. The villagers went back to the monk to acknowledge their mistake and inform him that the child's true father had returned. The monk again said little. Though he'd grown fond of the child, he returned it to its mother and father and resumed his monastic life.

If we have been misjudged, rather than attempting to defend ourselves or control how others perceive us, we do better to focus on our own actions and behavior. Instead of getting worked up, we can, with humility, put our full attention and energy into taking good care of whatever is presented to us.

16

Dogen's Instructions for Sitting Meditation

"For *zazen*, a quiet room is suitable. Eat and drink moderately. Cast aside all involvements and cease affairs. Do not think good or bad. Do not administer pros or cons. Cease all movements of the conscious mind, the gauging of all thoughts and views. Have no designs on becoming a buddha. [Zazen] has nothing whatever to do with sitting or lying down.

At the site of your regular sitting, spread out thick matting and place a cushion on top of it. Sit either in the full-lotus or half-lotus position: you first place your right foot on your left thigh, and then your left foot on your right thigh. In the half-lotus, you simply press your left foot against your right thigh. You should have your robes and belt loosely bound and arranged in order. Then place your right hand on your left leg, and your left palm [facing upward] on your right palm, thumb-tips touching.

Thus, sit upright in a correct bodily posture, neither inclining to the left nor to the right, neither leaning forward nor backward. Be sure your ears are on a plane with your shoulders, and your nose in line with your navel. Place your tongue against the front roof of your mouth, with teeth and lips both shut. Your eyes should always remain open, and you should breathe gently through your nose.

"Once you have adjusted your posture, take a deep breath, inhale and exhale, rock your body right and left and settle into a steady, immobile sitting position. Think of not-thinking. How do you think of not-thinking? Non-thinking. This in itself is the essential art of *zazen*."

—From Dogen's *Fukanzazengi* (*Universal Recommendation for Zazen*), translated by Norman Waddell and Abe Masao.

17

We Are Never Done

Through the practice of meditation we have the chance to wake up. We have the chance to step out of the prisons of habitual thoughts and actions that we have been trapped in. However, stepping out of the prison does not mean that the prison will just melt away, or that it will never reappear. We mustn't hold on to a fixed idea of freedom or release. If we think there's any sort of permanence to our freedom, we will get lost.

As we begin to experience the initial frontiers of awakening, we are touched by a feeling of liberation. We feel really good, we might even tell ourselves: "Wow, I will never go back there again. I'm no longer trapped by old patterns." Then later, without warning, we find ourselves back in the prison of our conditioned responses, of our old habits and tendencies. Then we ask ourselves with frustration, How did this happen?

We are always susceptible to the seduction of our suffering, of our conditioned nature. The treatment for these conditioned responses is the sustained, committed, disciplined practice of meditation—meditation rooted in the awareness that there is freedom from suffering. I don't have to be trapped in cycles of repetition. I don't have to wander aimlessly in dark, dusty realms. I can become more and more sensitive to how my mind works. I can become more and more sensitive to the nature and many expressions of my conditioning. In the place of awareness, I have choices that did not exist before.

18

Vigilance on the Path

f I embrace a disciplined spiritual practice rooted in self-reflection, I have real choices, I have freedom. I will be able to hear the faint but firm voice that directs and leads me, the gentle voice of wisdom. The more I commit myself to living in this way, breathing in and breathing out, the more my life shows me the path to take. But I always have to be alert, aware, constantly vigilant. I must always look deeply into the nature of my actions.

19

Working Meditation

Work is an essential part of our lives. It is an expression of our creativity and of our connect-edness with life. Whether in our workplace or at home, there are always things to be done, so we might as well use these tasks as opportunities to understand that meditation does not stop when we get up off our cushions.

The shortest instruction for working meditation is to stay connected with your breath as you work. As you do a task, whether it's cleaning the dishes, cutting the grass, or conducting a business meeting, take the time to notice all the details—how things look, feel, smell. Be aware of what you perceive to be pleasant or unpleasant. Notice all the thoughts, feelings, and sensations that arise as you work. Make an effort to notice where you are off balance in your work style and take a step towards more balance.

For example, if you are someone who always works alone, ask someone for help. If you keep yourself mostly to the side and let others take initiative, then be a little more assertive. If you have a tendency to work too quickly, slow down. In this way, our meditation practice can grow and develop throughout the day and become part of everything we do.

20

Meditation Is Not Medication

D o not be confused: Meditation is not medication. It will not rescue us from our pain, from unwanted mental or emotional states. Meditation is not for escaping our discomfort or for fixing ourselves. Meditation is about knowing more intimately that which we view as uncomfortable or unwanted. Please know that our discomfort does not mean that we are fundamentally broken, ill, or disordered. Discomfort is an unavoidable part of the human experience.

Meditation is about facing ourselves—about developing the courage and commitment to be present to our thoughts, feelings, and perceptions on an ongoing basis, no matter what we're doing. One of the primary ways to do this is to maintain awareness of the breath.

The path of meditation is about living life on life's terms rather than attempting to force life to conform to our terms or our ideas of how it ought to be. When we live this way, when we bring meditation practice into all aspects of our lives, we gradually come to discover our innate wisdom and our essential unbrokenness.

21

Physical Pain in Sitting Practice

I have been practicing sitting meditation, in one form or another, for more than four decades, and it wasn't until about ten years or so that I became able to sit without physical discomfort. But during those initial decades I continued to just sit and work with my body, allowing it to inform me. I experimented with different sitting positions: sitting in *seiza* (knees forward), on benches, in half-lotus. I tried all sorts of things over the years, and suddenly it just worked. I have no idea what happened. Something changed, and I could just sit for hours without any real difficulty.

But then a few years ago my knees needed surgery. Right after the surgery I could not do prostrations or sit on a cushion. I still don't have the flexibility that I had before the surgery, but I am now able to do prostrations, and I can sit on a cushion with some extra support for my knees.

If you experience pain during sitting meditation, it's important to listen to your body, letting go of fixed ideas of how things have to be. When I am thinking too much I cannot hear what my body is telling me. It's about really wanting to sit then listening and experimenting, finding out what works.

The whole process of waking up is rooted in truly wanting to live differently. It doesn't matter how strong the conditioning is or what the obstacles are. What matters is the desire. The wanting. Even with significant injuries, I have found a way, by listening to my body, because I want to live differently. I have no fixed idea about what living differently will mean, or what it might look like, none at all. It's always a process of listening and adjusting.

22

On Bowing

I n the first Zen monastery where I lived and studied, I was instructed in how and when to bow. I was told to press my palms together with my thumbs and fingertips touching. I was to then rest my thumbs on the knuckles of my index fingers, and the tips of my longest fingers were to be parallel with the tip of my nose. In Japanese, the name of this position is *gassho*.

The form was not to be too rigid or too relaxed. I was to place my hands at a comfortable distance from my body, not extended too far away nor too close. When bowing I was told to bow at the waist, keeping my eyes engaged with the person or object to which I was bowing. No other part of my body was to move.

Upon entering the meditation hall, I was instructed to step in with my right foot first and then bow in this manner to the space itself. I was then to go to my sitting place and bow toward my cushion and then to turn—never showing my back to the altar—and bow to the person sitting across from me. I was also instructed to bow when the teacher or person leading the practice period entered the meditation hall, which was announced with the sound of a bell.

At the time, I felt great resistance to all of this. I suffered immensely from my preconceived notions of what bowing represented. I thought bowing was an act of subjugation, a sign of being below another person. So I defiantly resisted following instructions. I stubbornly refused to bow to anyone or anything.

But one day, still consumed by my suffering, I entered the meditation hall and, looking around to make sure that I was not being observed, I half-heartedly bowed. I noticed that I did not feel diminished. I continued this half-hearted experiment in bowing until on one day, just before I entered the meditation hall, I heard a clear, calm inner voice encouraging me to let go of my resistance and just bow. I thought, *What's the harm. I can always stop.*

I placed my hands in *gassho*, as instructed, and I stepped into the meditation hall with my right foot first. At the moment that my left foot joined my right foot I bowed. When I stood upright again, I was flooded with a rush of feelings, and I burst into tears. I experienced a lightness of being that I did not know existed, a freedom from suffering that arose from bowing just to bow.

Since then I have come to appreciate the power of bowing practice in the process of waking up. It invites me to experience a powerful, sensitive, and engaged connection with whomever or whatever I am bowing to. I no longer see it as a gesture of submission—just the opposite. Today I see it as a way to honor the potential for awakening that exists in each and every one of us.

23

Practice for Everyone

"You can enjoy your practice, but practicing just for yourself is not good enough. If you practice just for yourself, you attach to the idea of getting something from practice. Then your expectations are endless, and you will never find peace. So your practice must be for everyone: you, other people, birds, trees, and all beings."

—**Dainin Katigiri**, *Each Moment Is the Universe*

24

Discipline

I f we truly want to pursue the path of meditation practice, we must develop discipline. Discipline arises out of the desire to live differently. If we don't really want to live differently, if we don't really want to wake up, if we are not willing to do whatever it takes, then nothing will really change. The press of our conditioning—of our ingrained habits of thought and action—is strong and seductive. Our minds will create all sorts of reasons, all sorts of justifications, to avoid a disciplined meditation practice.

I often encounter people who are in rather desperate life circumstances and they want these circumstances to change. I offer them the tools and instruction that were passed along to me, the tools of meditation and mindfulness, and then I listen and observe their response. Often these same people will tell me why they can't do what I have recommended, why they don't have the time or don't need to do what I've suggested. It is in this moment that I see the real nature and power of their conditioning and their suffering, and I know that this person is not yet ripe for practice or for healing and transformation.

With dedication I continue to point to the path of liberation from suffering. I have been given a map by my teachers. This map has been passed down through 83 generations of Buddhist teachers to me. It is the light at the tip of the candle, hot and bright, feeding me with energies that seem to be boundless. I notice that when I am in the presence of someone who is really serious about practice and change, I find renewed energy to teach and point the way. In these circumstances I will always give of my time and energies until the candle of my life is extinguished.

25

What Is Zen?

Zen is not about what we believe, what we think, or what we say. It's about what we do. It's about how we are in the world, how we interact with the people we come into contact with—those with whom we agree and those with whom we do not. It's about how we care for the objects that serve us in our daily lives, the sink, the stove, the shower, the toilet, the car. Zen is about the quality of attention that we bring to all aspects of our lives.

26

When the Path Gets Hard

When people begin to practice meditation, there is an initial emotional exhilaration that can come with those first brushes with the possibility of change. This emotionalism should not be mistaken for authentic spiritual practice or realization, though too often it is.

Meditation is the practice of awareness, of waking up, and at a certain point the practice will bring us to the place where we start to feel all the feelings that we have constructed our lives to avoid. At this point people often give up on spiritual practice, thinking that it's not working.

It's what we do at this critical juncture that will determine how our lives will continue to unfold. Will we choose to face our pain, to finally stop running away from it? Will we have the courage to step into our suffering? To develop and trust a disciplined practice supported by a community of like-minded people and an authentic teacher? Spiritual practice is hard work. It is not for the faint of heart. It's not a casual thing. So, in the end, the burning question is always, *What are you willing to do?*

27

Making Contact with Fear

The only way I can heal my wounds, the only way I can awaken, is to live in the present moment, breathing in and breathing out. Every time I come in contact with my fear, I must first learn to establish an open relationship with it, neither attaching to it nor rejecting it. Then the next step is to see what is behind this fear. It's like turning over stones. I must continue to turn over stones until the day I die, looking ever more deeply.

28

The Cause of Suffering

"It is not life that brings sorrow, but the demands we make on life. The cause of *dukkha* [unsatisfactoriness] is selfish desire: *trishna,* the thirst to have what one wants and to get one's own way. Thinking life can make them happy by bringing what they want, people run after the satisfaction of their desires. But they get only unhappiness, because selfishness can only bring sorrow.

There is no fire like selfish desire. Not a hundred years of experience can extinguish it, for the more you feed it, the more it burns. It demands what experience cannot give: permanent pleasure unmixed with anything unpleasant. But there is no end to such desires; that is the nature of the mind. Suffering because life cannot satisfy selfish desire is like suffering because a pear tree cannot grow grapes."

—**Eknath Easwaran**, from his introduction to the
  Dhammapada

29

Stop Blaming Others

We can't make the external world become peaceful; we can only become peace. This is the only way. There is so much trauma and sadness in the world, so much suffering. We need to be willing to look at it and at how we are responsible, how we contribute to this cycle. When we stop blaming others and begin looking deeply within ourselves, we can discover how suffering arises, how it is linked to violence, and how to stop the seemingly endless cycles of aggression.

30

Letting Go of Results

Please understand that when we engage in a sustained, committed spiritual practice, we cannot know the outcome or the results in advance. What we do know, however, is that if we don't commit ourselves to spiritual practice we will continue to perpetuate cycles of suffering in ourselves and in our world. Without knowing exactly what the results will be, we engage in meditation practice *just for the sake of it*. We choose to move in the direction of transformation and healing, knowing that we must let go of any preconceptions or ideas about the nature of transformation and healing.

31

Eating Meditation

We all have to eat, but we usually don't pay much attention to what we are eating or how we are eating it. Too often we absentmindedly shovel down our food while talking to someone or watching a screen, not fully tasting, savoring, or appreciating our food. Eating in this way keeps us out-of-touch with ourselves and can make food into a drug that we use to numb our feelings.

In eating meditation we bring our full awareness to the process of eating. When you sit down with a plate of food, before you start eating, pause and take three conscious breaths. Then recite this verse out loud or internally:

This food is the gift of the whole universe, the earth, the sky, and much hard work.

May we live in a way that makes us worthy to receive it.
May we transform our unskillful states of mind, especially our greed.
May we take only foods which nourish us and prevent illness.
We accept this food so that we may realize the path of practice: of love, compassion, and peace.

Then start eating. If possible, eat in silence. Chew each bite of food fifty times. The only thing that prevents us from doing this is swallowing the food too quickly. Many of us have the habit of immediately swallowing each mouthful after just one or two chews. It's as if we simply want to get it over with, in and down. Take your time to appreciate the wonderful gift of food, the smells, tastes, looks, and sounds.

Take fifteen minutes to practice eating meditation and your body will have a chance to let you know when you have eaten enough—a point that we often miss. At the end of the eating meditation, breathe in and out three times and say out loud or internally, "Thank you." Or, if you like, place your hands in *gassho* (palms pressed together) and use this closing verse:

May we exist in muddy water, with purity like the lotus.
Thus we bow to Buddha.

32

Your Life Is a Pivotal Opportunity

"You have gained the pivotal opportunity of human form. Do not use your time in vain. You are maintaining the essential working of the Buddha Way. Who would take wasteful delight in the spark from a flintstone? Besides, form and substance are like the dew on the grass, destiny like the dart of lightning—empty in an instant, vanished in a flash."

—From Dogen's *Fukanzazengi* (*Universal Recommendation for Zazen*), translated by Norman Waddell and Abe Masao.

33

No Intention

To engage in meditation practice it is critical to understand that there can be no intention, no goal, nothing in particular that we are trying to achieve. It's easy to get lost in all of our ideas about things, in our hopes and expectations, and miss the whole point of what it is that we are doing.

If I get too caught up in fixed ideas about posture, how long I should sit, and so forth, I may miss the point, and that is *just sitting*. My commitment need only be to sit just to sit, to walk just to walk, to eat just to eat, to breathe just to breathe. This is waking up. We practice just to practice, to slow down, to become the observer as well as the participant in the activities that make up our lives. The point of practice is to look and to see, to discover. Through discovery, awareness can grow.

34

What Is Loving?

A student once asked me, "What does it mean to be loving?" If we think that we know what loving is, for sure, those thoughts are not the truth of loving. It is only a view of love from a certain angle of perception, and that perception is rooted in our conditioning. Here is where we get into trouble. We have an idea of what loving is, which then sets in motion, either consciously or unconsciously, the effort to get life to conform to our idea.

It is so very important not to confuse our ideas of love with the truth of love. Through a sustained, committed meditation practice, we begin to notice more about ourselves and the world around us. We begin to discover what is or is not loving, beyond our fixed ideas, our expectations, and our conditioning. We must be prepared to discover that the truth of love or compassion, or whatever else, might not be anything like what we thought.

35

The Second Precept:
Do Not Steal

The precepts are not a set of rules to be followed rigidly but a set of guiding principles that support us in becoming more awake and aware in our lives. The second Buddhist precept asks us to commit ourselves to not stealing. I might think of myself as someone who has never stolen anything, but it's important to look beyond the obvious forms of stealing. For example, have I ever taken away someone's sense of well-being or security by being inconsiderate or unkind? Have I ever robbed someone of their chance to grow and develop emotionally, intellectually, professionally? Have I ever discriminated— whether consciously or unconsciously—on the basis of race, gender, sexual orientation, or religion? In what ways do I benefit from the exploitation of the environment? By developing a greater awareness of the ways I do in fact steal, I finally have the chance to stop and to begin to live differently.

36

As I Am, the World Becomes

One of the most important aspects of Buddhist teaching, at least for me, is the truth of interconnectedness: the truth that within me exists the entire universe, so, as I am, the world becomes. It is not my responsibility to change the world but to slow down, to invite more silence into my life, so that the truth of my own suffering can surface. This is something I can address.

Often when working with my own suffering, what's important is not what I do but rather what I stop doing. When my suffering shows itself, I can stop acting in automatic, habitual, or conditioned ways. I can pause and make new choices.

Life during Covid times demonstrates the reality of interconnectedness without question. My actions affect everybody I come into contact with. If I want the world to be different, then I need to live differently, regardless of what others are doing. I need to live purposefully, not rigidly, but with an awareness of consequences. If I go out in society and behave carelessly, sooner or later I am going to bump into someone who has the virus. Then when I become sick, I impact everyone around me. The thought of this brings me in contact with a sense of discomfort. This discomfort is not really because of the external circumstances. Likewise, the solution to my discomfort is not external. We have been given a great opportunity in this situation to wake up to our discomfort and to begin to live differently. We have no choice but to confront the truth of interconnectedness.

37

Study the Self

often speak about the four essentials of Zen practice: silence, discipline, ritual, and study. When I mention study, most people immediately think about which books they need to read. They have an academic or intellectual association with the word "study." I understand that, but the sense of "study" that has been conveyed to me is not limited to an intellectual pursuit. Study includes the intellect, however, study also includes the attention we pay to our thoughts, the attention we pay to our feelings, and the attention we pay to our perceptions as we move through our day. Zen practice is about being willing to study ourselves, to wake up to the causes and conditions that keep us trapped in cycles of suffering.

38

The Mind in Meditation

Many people are under the impression that meditation is about eliminating our thoughts, about somehow stopping them or clearing the mind. When entering into an active engagement with meditation, it's important not to cling to some idea or goal that we then chase after. We just sit in an upright position, place our awareness on our breath, and pay attention to what happens.

By "paying attention" I am not talking about some kind of concentrated, intellectual way of paying attention. The paying attention that I am referring to here is more like sitting on a bench at a busy park or city square observing what happens. Watching just to watch, watching all the things that happen.

When you sit, notice not only what you perceive with your senses, but how your intellect processes this information. Don't hold too tightly to this information or the conclusions that the intellect begins to draw. Pay attention but don't grasp at anything.

Remain open and curious. Notice sensations, judgments, attachments, and how the intellect grabs at these experiences and attempts to convince us of the absoluteness of all of its positions. I may not have much awareness right away. But, if I continue to sit and stay concentrated on my breath, my awareness will grow. So please understand that sitting meditation is fundamentally about paying attention, and the breath is simply a tool that can support this process. There are no particular goals.

39

True Bowing

"Dogen Zenji once said: 'As long as there is true bowing, the Buddha Way will not deteriorate.' In bowing, we totally pay respect to the all-pervading virtue of wisdom, which is the Buddha.

In making the bow, we should move neither hastily nor sluggishly but simply maintain a reverent mind and humble attitude. When we bow too fast, the bow is then too casual a thing; perhaps we are even hurrying to get it over and done with. This is frequently the result of a lack of reverence.

On the other hand, if our bow is too slow, then it becomes a rather pompous display; we may have gotten too attached to the feeling of bowing, or our own (real or imagined) gracefulness of movement.

This is to have lost the humble attitude which a true bow requires."

—**Taizan Maezumi Roshi**, *On Zen Practice*

40

The Third Precept:
Sexual Clarity

The third Buddhist precept addresses the topic of sexuality and chaste conduct. In our lineage, during the precept ceremony, the teacher asks the student, "As buddhas, throughout all space and time, have encountered all creations with respect and dignity, will you vow to give and accept affection and friendship without clinging? This is the precept of sexual clarity." This precept provides us with the opportunity to explore the nature of intimacy—with oneself and others. Am I able to have intimate, vulnerable, and caring relationships with others without automatically converting that into sexual craving and conquest?

It's important to make a distinction between our human sexuality and the sex act. Because I am human, I have biological urges and conditioned responses. I don't deny the existence of these impulses, but I also don't allow my impulses and conditioning to dictate my actions.

41

Meditation Is Not
Stress-Reduction

Often people get seduced into the idea that they should sit in meditation for long periods of time. Perhaps they find a certain comfort in this idea. But this is more often than not a way of using sitting meditation as an anesthetic, an escape from our suffering.

Meditation is not fundamentally about stress-reduction, even though it does get marketed this way. Meditation is about much more than this. The disciplined practice of meditation is about transforming ourselves and our world. In truth, sitting on a cushion is like sitting on a bomb. As we become more still, all of the suffering that we have carefully kept out of our awareness, through all of our action and activity, will begin to surface. At times it might even explode into our awareness. If we continue to practice sitting meditation at this key point, we will learn how to be present with all of this. We'll learn how to be at peace with our unpeacefulness, how to develop steadiness and awareness under any circumstances.

42

Don't Indulge Illusions

"Deluded people don't realize that their own mind is the Buddha. They keep searching outside. They never stop invoking buddhas or worshipping buddhas and wondering, *Where is the Buddha*? Don't indulge in such illusions. Just know your mind. Beyond your mind there's no other buddha. The sutras say, 'Everything that has form is an illusion.' They also say, 'Wherever you are, there's Buddha.'"

—*The Zen Teachings of Bodhidharma*, translated by Red Pine

43

When Practice "Doesn't Work"

When we first discover meditation practice, there's usually a period of excitement. We think, *I've found the answer!* But soon the elation wears off, and after a period of time most people give up, thinking that meditation doesn't work. They still get angry, feel restless, have trouble sleeping. Many of us hold a false expectation that meditation should make all of our uneasiness disappear; all our stress, anxiety, and sleeplessness ought to simply vanish. However, the truth is that awakening is not the absence of suffering. Awakening is about learning to live in a different and more conscious relationship with our suffering so that it no longer dominates our lives and drives our choices.

44

Recognizing Our Conditioning

Sitting meditation is one of the tools that we use to become more aware of how our thought processes, our emotional responses, and our perceptions are influenced by our conditioning. By "conditioning" I mean the unspoken education we have received, the messages and attitudes we picked up from our families, our communities, and our society.

For example, I am a white male who was raised in a rural community in northwestern Pennsylvania. I was conditioned by my environment and, by the larger society of which I am a part, to be racist and sexist. Meditation practice has helped me to recognize this conditioning and how it shows up in my daily life, in my thoughts, feelings, and actions. Zen practice has allowed me to develop a more conscious relationship with this conditioning. Meditation does not make my racism or sexism go away, but it does start to transform as I become more conscious of it and able to make new choices.

45

Bow to Realize the Truth

"Constantly try to realize the depth of human life. Accept the fact that whatever you do, wherever you live, under all circumstances, you have a chance to realize the truth. When you bow in gassho [with palms together], just do gassho through and through. If you really do this, you can touch the ultimate truth. Then through gassho you learn something!"

—**Dainin Katigiri**, *Each Moment is the Universe*

46

The Frontiers of Awareness

I n sitting meditation we embark toward the frontiers of awareness, the place where we begin to put to rest our dependence on intellectual understanding, on words and speech. We take what might seem like a backward step, turning the light of awareness around to illuminate ourselves. Ultimately we develop the discipline to let body and mind just drop away. It is through a disciplined sitting practice that our original face can become manifest, the expression of self that is not created by the intention to shape perceptions. This is the expression of self that is willing to just sit still and observe, becoming aware of the systems of thought and behavior that are not supportive of living in harmony with the interconnected reality of which we are a part.

47

We Need the Support of a Sangha and a Teacher

When we establish a sustained, disciplined and committed sitting practice, we begin the process of training the mind, helping it to become right-sized. At the heart of practice is a willingness to allow the mind and emotions to manifest in an unfettered way. It is critically important to engage in this practice with the support of a group of like-minded people (a sangha) that is supported directly by an authentic teacher, someone who has traveled this path ahead of you, someone who is well trained in an established tradition. It is dangerous to go forward independently, without a community and a teacher. People who engage with the practice of sitting meditation often underestimate its power.

When we sit engaged in slow, steady, rhythmic breathing, the processes of the mind slow down and, in an instant, it is possible that you can fall right through yourself. Unprepared (if ever one can be prepared for such an experience) or unaware of what is happening, lacking the skills to navigate such an experience, this can be a great shock. If there is no one to turn to, or if there is no one around to recognize what is happening and to offer guidance and support, great harm can be the end result. Take care, don't go it alone.

48

Idealizing the Teacher

"Students almost always create an idealistic image of their spiritual teacher. The teacher should always be calm, should not show emotion, and of course should never get angry. They should not make any errors and never take back today what was said yesterday.

They are not allowed to become sick and are definitely not allowed to die, or if they die, then they are not permitted to do so until at least the age of 120 (as the teacher always needs to be there for *you*). They are not allowed to sit in front of the television screen, and for sure they are not allowed to watch the programs that you consider to be of poor quality.

They must know about everything that is happening in the world. They are not allowed to have faults, or what *you* consider to be faults. In short, students create a caricature, a god-like image, and are shocked when this person doesn't conform to this image.

It is even worse when students claim that their teacher is exactly like the god image they've created in their imaginations, and even worse than that when they attach themselves to this dream even after the teacher's death. These students take away the dignity of their teachers."

—Author unknown. From the German publication *Zen*, No. 31, 1996. Translated by Wiebke KenShin Beckmann-Andersen.

49

Don't Reject Negative Voices or Sensations

There are voices within me today that still tell me that I am useless and worthless because of where I come from and what I have done. Those voices never go away. However, I have come to a place where I don't want or need them to go away. Without them I wouldn't be the person I am, and I wouldn't have the opportunities that I have today. They are actually a great support to me. These voices help me to stay right-sized, to understand that I am not as wonderful nor as terrible as some people or situations might suggest.

Likewise, the pain that I experience in my body when I do sitting meditation is not something unwanted. It's information. How do I work with that? What adjustments do I need to make? What is the situation telling me? This is always the point. How do I work with my discomfort directly?

50

Breath Awareness in Meditation

I n sitting meditation, pay attention to the precise point where the breath enters the body. Don't follow it all the way into your body, just bring your attention to the point of entry and the point of exit of the breath. It's about gaining some degree of focus and then noticing where the distractions are. Notice the distractions and just let them go. Letting distractions go does not mean they stop or disappear from our practice. It means our relationship to them changes. We learn to notice when we are distracted and simply return our attention to the breath.

51

I Have to Be Willing to Be Uncomfortable

I f I want to wake up and experience life directly, I have to be willing to be uncomfortable. We live in a society that tells us to avoid any sensation, feeling, or experience categorized as "uncomfortable" or "unpleasant." We are encouraged not to be sad, lonely, confused, or frustrated, to name a few of these feelings. We need to learn to become at peace with what we have been conditioned to experience as our unpeacefulness. It is in the heart of our unpeacefulness that we can discover the true nature of a balanced life lived directly, with all its joys and sorrows.

52

Life is Meditation Practice

A sustained, disciplined practice does not only take the form of sitting meditation. Sitting practice is the root, the foundation. We have to see how this root then grows into everything that we do in our daily lives. Daily life and spiritual practice are not two separate things. Work and meditation are not different. Eating and meditation are not different. The point is to realize that our life is meditation. There is not anything other than or separate from this.

53

Swept Away by Thoughts

When we do sitting meditation, we begin to see when our thoughts just sweep us away. We usually begin a period of sitting with strong focus on the breath. Then time passes and we notice: *Oh, the breath! What happened to my breath?* In these moments of awareness you know you have been swept away by thoughts. It happens to everyone, including me. Over time, we can bring this same kind of awareness of our mind and its distractions into all aspects of our lives, no matter what we're doing. We do this by grounding all our activities in an awareness of the breath and then noticing how our attention gets pulled away.

The point is not to give up. You cannot realize the benefits of practice unless you persist. Even when the mind says: "What are you doing? This is just a waste of time."

Doubts will arise. These doubts will then give birth to a myriad of reasons not to continue with practice. It is precisely in these moments that it is important to just continue to practice in relation with your doubt, with all the questions born out of your doubt, and see what happens.

Impatience is a great sickness of Western culture, of all contemporary societies—impatience and a sense of entitlement to an easy solution. If something doesn't work right away, doesn't show results, we're done. People think, "I've practiced meditation for a month, and it's not working. It's useless. I'll go do something else." Practice does not work like that. Practice requires a sustained, disciplined commitment. Please stay with it.

54

The Fourth Precept: Do Not Lie

When we take the fourth Buddhist precept, we vow to "speak the truth and deceive no one" and to "see and act in accordance with what is." Here we are guided to explore the difference between being lovingly honest and brutally frank. If I see someone in the grocery store who's overweight, this precept does not give me permission to walk up to them and say, "You're fat." It does encourage me to be more conscious of my conditioned reactions to what I define as being different or to what doesn't conform to my ideas of what is correct.

This precept also guides us to explore the difference between the honesty that exists in the relative world described above—the realm of right/wrong, good/bad, yes/no—and the honesty that can be experienced in the absolute realm which lies beyond such distinctions and separations.

This precept is also about living our practice openly and out loud, resisting the impulse to hide our spiritual commitments.

55

No Gain

With sitting meditation, there is nothing to be accomplished, nothing to be gained. We sit just to sit. We don't need to think too much about this. We just concentrate on the breath, and when we become distracted, we come back to an awareness of our breathing.

Thoughts can be an inexpensive form of entertainment, more interesting than movies and television at times. If I don't act on them, they don't cost me anything. If I take my thoughts too seriously and act on them, they can cost me a great deal.

56

Unusual Experiences
in Meditation

Several years ago, while in Italy leading a period of sitting practice, I had an unusual experience. I heard a clear voice that began telling me a story, "You were a soldier in Vietnam. You were seriously wounded. As a result of your wounds, you have been in a coma. Everything you are experiencing right now is unreal." And then the voice asked, "Do you want to wake up?" and I thought, *I don't know*. I hesitated. I thought about my life as I was experiencing it, and I liked the way it was unfolding. But since that day, every now and then, I have a bit of regret that I did not say yes to see what happened next, if anything.

Things like this can happen in meditation. It is important to not take sitting practice lightly, and to be in contact with an experienced, authentic teacher so that when things like this arise, and they will, there is a trusted person to speak with about the experience.

57

Act Carefully and You Won't Miss

"Ying Shaowu said to Master Zhenjing Wen:

Whatever is rushed to maturity will surely break down early. Whatever is accomplished in a hurry will surely be easily destroyed. What is done without making consideration for the long run, and is hastily finished, is not of a far reaching and great character.

Now sky and earth are most miraculous, but still it is only after three years and two intercalary months that they complete their accomplishment and fulfill their transformations. How much the more so for the miracle of the Great Way—how could it be easily mastered? It is essential to build up achievement and accumulate virtue. Therefore it is said, 'When you want to be quick, you don't succeed; act carefully and you won't miss.'

"A beautiful accomplishment takes a long time, ultimately involving lifelong consideration. A sage said, 'Keep it with faith, practice it with keenness, perfect it with faithfulness—then though the task be great, you will surely succeed.'"

—*Zen Lessons*, translated by Thomas Cleary

58

How to Recognize an
Authentic Teacher

M any people have been to a couple of meditation retreats, have read a couple of books, and think they suddenly have all the answers. And there are a lot of people who will gravitate toward someone like this out of a desire to be told what to do or to be permitted to do whatever they want.

An authentic teacher rarely commands. He or she points students in a direction. He or she adjusts your posture, encourages you to be on time, reminds you of the importance of silence, of sitting just to sit, of working just to work, or suggests that it is time to take the next step, such as ordination. A trustworthy teacher is someone who recommends practices and steps, but doesn't seek to control you, and is someone who doesn't claim to know more than they do. He or she is someone who is there primarily as a guide and who, rather than drawing attention and adulation to themselves, always points students back to the path.

59

The World Is
Communicating to Us

The world is constantly communicating with us, but if we only listen for what we want to hear, then we miss so much of what life is saying, of what the world is showing us.

Perhaps you've heard that still, small voice telling you that it would be better not to say something, but you didn't listen and not listening led to more suffering. That's certainly happened to me. That still, small voice is the voice of awareness. Our habit of clinging to our ideas and expectations makes us ignore the voice of awareness and what life itself is telling us. It is this attachment to preconceptions and selfish desires that keeps us trapped in endless cycles of suffering.

60

Facing Our Feelings

The first few years of meditation practice were challenging for me because of some of the feelings that would rise up. I sometimes felt like I might explode. In the past, intense feelings controlled me, and I always reacted to them by trying to escape them. I took drugs, got into fights, drove too fast, spent too much money, got involved with too many women. These were all attempts to avoid strong, uncomfortable feelings. However, once I began to practice meditation, when those intense feelings came up, I learned to just sit still and breathe. With time, my relationship to these feelings started to change. It took time, but I began to sit with them without expecting that these feelings would go away. In reality, they don't have to go away for us to find healing and peace.

61

Not Knowing

When we sit in silence, we make contact with the reality of not knowing. This is the place where we have the opportunity to let go of resistance, where we have the opportunity to stop fighting the truth of what is. Most of us have been conditioned to fear not knowing, but in Zen teaching this is the hallmark of the awakened mind.

62

Each Sitting Is Different

Each period of meditation is different for me. What remains constant is concentrating on my breath, and sometimes I still wonder about this. I think, "What is the value of just placing my awareness on the breath?"

Thoughts like this come and go. There is no correct or ideal experience when we practice meditation. There is only the presentness that can exist in an active meditation practice. It is the craving after some ideal that keeps us from being present. When sitting in meditation there is only noticing, without rejecting and without attaching. There is only the knowing that there is nothing to be achieved, nothing to be gained. Just stay in contact with the breath and pay attention.

63

I Am Responsible

Through Buddhist practice I have come to understand that I am responsible for my life and that every action has a consequence, though I cannot know in advance what that consequence will be. The best use of my life is to concentrate wholeheartedly on waking up to the reality of life. To be willing to experience the truth of interconnectedness, that I am not separate from all that is, and to become conscious of the causes and conditions of my life.

64

Facing Our Aggression

I have been conditioned to react to feelings of fear and powerlessness with aggression. This aggression can express itself differently depending on the situation. In some situations this aggression can manifest as silence, the withholding of kindness or affection. In other situations this aggression can express itself through emotional explosiveness (rage), which can take the form of violence against myself, violence against the other, or violence against inanimate objects (punching holes in the wall, throwing objects, breaking things). But through an unwavering commitment to living differently, supported by a disciplined spiritual practice rooted in self-reflection, I have discovered that I can live in a more conscious relationship with how my conditioned behaviors have shaped my life.

If we really want to live differently, we can. If we want the world to be different, it is not a question of changing the political system or correcting social injustice. These are valuable and important, but until we finally face the seeds of war and violence within ourselves, nothing will really change, we will not put an end to war and suffering. We must stop fighting the endless wars that rage within.

65

Moving beyond Our
Ideas of Things

Spiritual practice is hard work. Waking up is not a comfortable process. Turning the light inward breaks down our defenses. You have to want to look at yourself—not at the idea of yourself, but at your actual self, your lived experience. You have to be willing to look and to see. You also have to be willing to sit in the reality of not knowing.

The purpose of a disciplined meditation practice is to let go—to let go of all ideas, expectations, attachments, and just deal with what is presented in the moment. Living in this way is living the reality of life, living in the unknown, allowing the unknown to become our teacher.

66

Birth and Death Are Constantly Occurring

"One understanding of life and death is the life and death of the instant. According to Dogen Zenji, the founder of Japanese Soto Zen, Shakyamuni Buddha said that in twenty-four hours our life is born and dying, rising and falling, 6,400,099,980 times. So in one second, our life is born and dies around seventy thousand times. Our conscious mind cannot even imagine such an occurrence. What kind of life is this?

We usually think of our life as fifty years, sixty years, maybe at the most around one hundred years. Dogen Zenji said that living a long life without awareness is almost a crime. On the contrary, he emphasized that even if you live one day with a clear understanding of what life is, the value of that one day is equal to many, many years of living without awareness.

We must see our life clearly. The existence of this life at this very moment, what is it? Being born and dying seventy thousand times at this very moment—what is it?"

—**Taizan Maezumi Roshi**, *Appreciate Your Life*

67

When I See Injustice
in the World

When I see abuse, neglect, disinformation, or downright untruths being perpetuated in the world around me, the answer is not to appease those responsible or to excuse or accept injustice. At the same time, I am committed to not treating anyone as an enemy. I must, in these circumstances, continue to live a life rooted in a disciplined spiritual practice, striving to know myself more intimately. This process will grow and bring me into a more meaningful and consistent contact with reality—the interconnected reality of which I am a part. If I am patient with this process, in time, what actions I should take will be revealed to me.

68

The Fifth Precept:
Abstaining from Intoxicants

I n our lineage, the text of the fifth precept reads, "As buddhas throughout all space and time have cultivated a mind that sees clearly, I vow to abstain from using intoxicants, or encouraging others to do so, and to embrace all experience directly." This precept encourages us to notice our tendency to distract ourselves from the truth of existence.

On the path of practice, of waking up, it is imperative to abstain from consuming any mood-altering or mind-altering substances, legal or illegal, including alcohol, marijuana, and nicotine. Once we develop the courage to start experiencing life more directly, this percept will then guide us toward discovering the less obvious intoxicants that we might gravitate toward: work, food, caffeine, relationships, shopping, even meditation itself can be used to avoid or escape our lived experience. Any time I view the source of my salvation or my relief as external to myself, I'm in danger of being seduced into the realm of delusion, which can lead to a dependence on intoxicants.

69

There Are No Evil People

There are no inherently evil people. We all have the capacity within us to commit evil actions. We're in trouble if we don't know this. Many of us who have served in war have touched the truth of our potential for evil. This is the reason that I continue to assert that war is merely the collective expression of individual suffering, that the roots of all wars, of all evil, are personal and therefore resolvable providing that we, individually, are willing to address the roots of war, violence, and suffering that we carry.

We must wake up to this potential to do evil that is within us all. We must then put forth all of our effort to not reject or deny this aspect of our selves and to not let it control us. Then and only then will we be able to have the organic experience of peace with our unpeacefulness—not just the superficial, intellectual understanding of peace, but true healing and transformation.

70

Observing Ourselves

Each and every facet of our existence presents us with an opportunity to practice, to know ourselves more intimately, to recognize the conditioned way in which we perceive and respond to the world. This (our conditioned responses) is what we call "self." In time, through committed practice, we are better able to observe this self, to notice how it operates and then see the opportunities to make new choices.

71

On Falling in Love

More often than not, what we call "falling in love" is an illusion born of our desire to find something fixed, steady, and unchanging outside of ourselves that we can latch on to. It's often a craving for someone to take care of us, to provide us with some sense of safety and security, or simply for the thrill of the pursuit.

When it comes to relationships, there is also the great push to fulfill the social contract, the unspoken press of our society's norms. I am supposed to fall in love. I am not supposed to be alone. I am supposed to start a family. If I don't comply with this social contract, then something is wrong with me. I am deficient.

The most intimate relationships, however, can have little to do with conventional ideas of love, relationship, or sexuality. I can only discover what love is by waking up to the truth of how I have been conditioned and then being willing to live in a different, more conscious relationship with all of this.

72

Suffering Is Not Our Enemy

S ociety teaches us that suffering is our enemy. We are
constantly encouraged to reject what is unpleasant,
disappointing, or difficult. But our suffering is not
our enemy. It is only through a more conscious relationship with my pain, my sadness, that I can truly know and
touch the opposite, which is my pleasure, my joy, and my
happiness. We must change our attitudes toward our suffering, bringing an attitude of active nonviolence to our
daily experiences and to our world. We don't need to fight
or extinguish our suffering. We can meet it with openness,
honesty, and nonaggression.

73

Don't Expect Anything

"Master Obaku, the teacher of Master Rinzai, was famous for his frequent admonition to his students, 'Don't expect anything from the Three Treasures [the Buddha, the dharma, the sangha].' Time after time he was heard to say this. One day, however, Master Obaku was observed in the act of bowing and was challenged about this practice.

'You always tell your students not to expect anything from the Three Treasures,' said the questioner, 'and yet you have been making deep bows.' In fact, he had been bowing [full prostrations] so frequently and for so long that a large callous had formed on his forehead at the point where it touched the hard floor.

When asked how he explained this, Master Obaku replied, 'I don't expect. I just bow.'"

—**Taizan Maezumi Roshi**, *On Zen Practice*

74

Not Separate or Special

A life rooted in spiritual practice does not use that spiritual practice to create a sense of separateness or specialness. It does not use that spiritual practice for profit or gain. An authentic spiritual practice is not used as an identity, and it does not put us above anyone else. Instead, our practice leads us to see how we are connected with other people, with animate as well as inanimate existence. A disciplined spiritual practice helps us to see what we have in common, where we connect, how we are the same.

75

Active Nonviolence

Many people continue to believe that in certain circumstances we should kill to prevent further killing. My hope is to help people to discover what a terribly dangerous argument this is. This very argument has been used to justify preemptive strikes, to maintain a nuclear arsenal that could destroy the planet many times over, to uphold the death penalty. I know, unwaveringly, that violence is never the solution to humanity's problems, and that the real solution resides in the ethic and value of active nonviolence.

Active nonviolence means that I am aware that in any given situation I have the capacity to act violently, but that I have a commitment not to succumb to my conditioning, not succumb to my sense of helplessness that leads me, again and again, either actively or passively, to support

the use of violence to resolve conflicts. Active nonviolence means strongly standing up for truth and compassion in the midst of conflict and confrontation, without
aggression.

76

The Calm of
Meditation Practice

Many people believe that meditation practice will help them to become calmer. Here is the beginning of a problem. People tend to hold a particular view of what it means to be calm. They want to become more placid, to reach a state where they transcend the way they feel or simply don't feel so much. Awakening has nothing to do with this sort of calmness. Calmness can be a by-product of an active, engaged meditation practice, however, this calm is beyond our idea of it—beyond any idea.

Through a disciplined and consistent meditation practice we can develop greater stability and steadiness. This is not a state of having no unease, but a state of remaining rooted in practice in the midst of strong feelings or unsettling experiences. We can learn to stop being swept away by our emotional responses. With determination and commitment, we can discover how to live at peace with our unpeacefulness.

When we are fully engaged in a disciplined practice— rooted in breath awareness and self-reflection, supported by an authentic teacher and a community of like-minded people—we will wake up to a full range of feelings. Over time, our relationship to our feelings and impulses will begin to shift and transform, and we will discover new choices and new freedom.

77

Walking Meditation

Walking meditation is similar to sitting meditation, with the difference that we are now connecting our breath with our footsteps. With each in-breath we take a step with our right foot, and with each out-breath we take a step with our left foot. We walk slowly and deliberately, allowing a harmonious relationship to develop between our steps and our breath.

During walking meditation, find a comfortable position for your hands, such as clasped in front or behind your body. If you are in a group, walk in a line, one behind the other. Lower your gaze and let it rest in front of you. Be aware of your feet touching the floor as you walk, making contact with the earth with each step.

When we do walking meditation, we are not trying to get anywhere or accomplish anything. There is no goal and no destination. We are walking just to walk. When our mind wanders off, we bring our attention back to our steps and our breath.

It can be helpful to incorporate walking meditation into your daily life, for example, doing it each day on the way to work or school can help settle the mind and can create a restorative transition. Just slow down, pay attention to your breath and your steps. You are walking in the here and now. Especially in times of upset and worry, walking meditation is a wonderful tool to help us stay centered and not get carried away by our thoughts and feelings.

78

Facing Uncertainty

The truth of our existence is that it is uncertain. We create so much suffering and chaos by resisting this fact and by craving the security of a fixed point. We become desperate to make the world conform to our ideas and expectations so as to avoid feeling uneasy. But the reality of uncertainty, of not knowing, keeps showing itself. We fear the tension and anxiety this creates within us. We don't want to feel this. The practice of meditation—a consistent, dedicated practice—supports us in facing the feelings that rise up in response to life's uncertainty. Over time we develop acceptance of the fundamental uncertainty of our lives and the reality of not knowing.

79

Doubt Is Important

"Sometimes we think doubt is not good, but doubt is important. We need to question. Even though you don't get answers to your questions, all you have to do is just swim. Questioning is always going on in real time, it is always returning to zero. So, little by little, questioning becomes questionless."

—**Dainin Katigiri**, *Each Moment Is the Universe*

80

Deep Listening

So much of our suffering gets acted out in the ways that we communicate with each other and in the ways we listen—or fail to do so. The essence of deep listening is:

1. To be aware of what I feel as I listen to others speak;

2. To know that my feelings are my own and not necessarily those of the speaker;

3. To recognize that it is not my responsibility to fix, comfort, or heal the other person.

4. To understand that most communication is nonverbal.

With this approach, real listening becomes possible.

In our Zen lineage, we regularly recite the invocation of Avalokiteshvara, the bodhisattva who became enlightened

by hearing "the sounds of the world." This text empha-
sizes the value and importance of deep listening.

*We evoke your name, Avalokiteshvara. We aspire to
learn your way, which is to listen in order to lessen
the suffering in the world. You know how to listen in
order to understand.... We shall sit and listen without
any prejudice. We shall sit and listen without judging
and without reacting.... We shall practice listening so
attentively that we are able to hear what the other is
saying and also what is left unsaid. We know that just
by listening deeply we already alleviate a great deal of
the pain and suffering in the other.*

Learning to listen in this way is an essential aspect of
bringing meditation off the cushion and into our everyday lives. As with all forms of practice, this is an ongoing,
open-ended process. We can begin by noticing what gets
in the way of listening deeply. Am I missing what's being
said because I'm planning what I want to say? Am I thinking about how to fix or rescue the other person? If I notice
that I'm doing any of that, I can stop, consciously bring
my attention back to my breath, and just listen.

81

Impermanence

Life is fluid. Suffering comes when we attempt to attach fixed ideas to the fluid, unfixed process that is life.

Everything—absolutely everything—that comes into existence will pass away. Keep this in mind and do not waste one precious moment, because with each breath we sit at the edge of existence. We must live full and committed lives while at the same time not holding on too tightly.

Each evening we recite a verse that reminds us of the essential truth of impermanence:

Let me respectfully remind you:
Life and death are of supreme importance.
Time passes swiftly by and opportunity is lost.
Each of us must strive to awaken.
Awaken! Take heed! Do not squander this life!

82

On Fear

The only effective antidote to fear is the willingness to surrender and trust the practice that is our daily life. Through this process, life may not measure up to my expectations, however, with the support of my spiritual practice and my community, what I used to define as intolerable has much less sway. I am more able to be present through all of the realities that life offers up. I am more able to live in balance with my successes as well as those circumstances that don't work out the way that I would prefer. Rooted in a disciplined practice, I can choose not to fight with reality. I can learn to live in a more open and accepting relationship with it. The choice is mine.

A student asked me, "But what if there's a tragic outcome?" Our sense of what is tragic depends on our angle of perception. Yes, something might happen that we perceive to be tragic. We might experience a great loss. In these moments, our practice is to feel these feelings fully. It is also our practice not to add the idea of "tragic." We just continue to practice in the face of whatever we feel and whatever happens in our lives.

83

Taking Care of My Life

"It is not to profit personally or to become famous that we take good care of things, devote ourselves to our work, love those whom we encounter, or demonstrate our concern for social problems. When I take care of my own life, I take care of the world as my own life. I do this moment by moment, and in each situation, I enable the flower of my life to bloom."

—**Kosho Uchiyama**, *Opening the Hand of Thought*

84

Facing Our Own Potential for Violence

War puts soldiers in a position to kill, to act violently, but everyone has that same potential. We can pretend that we're not violent, that we would never be able to do what soldiers do—or what some gang members do, or what overly aggressive police officers do. Whenever we are confronted with violence, we as individuals and as a society can react in horror, attempt to hide from it, ignore it, or push it away as someone else's problem. But we need to touch this violent part of ourselves, recognizing that we *are* capable of violence—if we were to find ourselves in similar circumstances.

If we don't own our own complicity in the many wars that are being fought around the world, in our communities, and in our families, then we will continue to be trapped in the never ending cycle of war, violence, and suffering.

85

There Is No Safety in Silence

We may think there is some safety in keeping silent, keeping the story of our trauma to ourselves, but there isn't any safety in that. None. If we keep these stories to ourselves, or if we keep the most important parts of our stories to ourselves, that doesn't mean that people won't know about them or that they won't affect us. We have the ability to pierce the darkness of denial: our society's and our own. We have to speak and tell our stories.

86

Awareness of Every Action

To live in the present moment and find peace in our lives, we need to be mindful in all that we do, in every action that we take: the way we open the door, the way we put the dish on the shelf, the way we do our work, the way we talk to another person, the way we tie our shoes, take a step, stand up, sit down, brush our teeth, drive the car. It is not always easy. We are easily distracted by our thoughts, images of the past and the future, our dreams, our hopes, our regrets. It is here, at this point, this exact point of one breath, the present moment, that I have the freedom of choice to act differently, to not simply react as I have in the past.

87

I Went to My Teacher

"I went to my teacher with nothing and came away with nothing. Someone asked, 'Why bother to go to the teacher then?' The reply was, 'How otherwise would I know that I went with nothing and came away with nothing?'"

—**Albert Low**, *The Iron Cow of Zen*

88

Wanting to Forget

I spent most of my life living in a state of wanting to forget, of wanting to escape. Sometimes when I wake up in the morning, I am consumed by suffering, full of fear, full of doubts, full of shame. But now, rather than wanting to forget, I feel this shame as a bell of mindfulness. I breathe in and breathe out, and I am grateful to be free to touch these emotions, to establish a different relationship with them, to be able to have the possibility to make different choices in my life. When I live in wanting to forget, I have no choices. My conditioned nature is deciding for me.

89

Coming Back to the Breath

There are many voices, both within me and in the world, that try to distract me from waking up to the conditioned realities that are my suffering. When I hear the sound of the bell inviting me to attention, and I come back to my breath, these distractions become weaker. My breath quiets them. Then my suffering can show itself. I can touch it, allow it to emerge into my conscious awareness. I am no longer so tempted to hide from it or to drown in it.

With a commitment to live in a different relationship with my suffering, I am invited to touch it, to embrace it, without judging it. My thoughts, feelings, and perceptions are neither right nor wrong, good nor bad; they simply are. Without judgement, there is much more freedom in my life.

If we live our lives rooted in meditation practice, the moment will come when we are not controlled by our desperation, when we are no longer driven by the seductions of our suffering, because all experience becomes an act of meditation. Life becomes clearer, more fluid, more simple.

90

I Would Rather Have Not Killed

was a soldier in the Vietnam War. I would rather have not killed, but I have killed. And to reject that is to reject myself and the reality of my actions. Through meditation practice, through living in the present moment, I'm able to invite my whole self into my life, to integrate all the different parts of myself into one whole. Yes, I am the little boy playing baseball, and I am the soldier killing. Yes, I am the drug addict using heroin, and I am the father of a wonderful boy. I am all these things, and I must not turn away from any of them. As I welcome all of these elements of myself into the present moment, I am able to participate more fully in my life.

91

Our Lives Ripple Outward

Our lives are like stones thrown into a pond. When the stone enters the water, the ripples expand outward and change the whole pond. Likewise, if we live in forgetfulness, in non-mindfulness, our suffering will spread out and fill the pond. But if we live with an unwavering commitment to waking up, our healing will instead spread outward and eventually touch everything.

If I realize the teaching of interconnectedness, then I can come to a place of understanding—a place beyond the intellect. A place where I am not separate from anything. And here I will discover that I have an impact, that my actions have an impact on the whole world.

92

Trusting Others

used to think that trust was an all-or-nothing proposition. I either trusted you or I didn't. If I trusted you, then I needed to tell you everything. And if you trusted me, you would tell me everything. This was a misunderstanding. Today I begin with an attitude of trust, then I allow time to reveal the limits of trust between myself and another person. I find that I can trust different people in different ways with different things. There's no one person whom I trust completely or with everything. I've also found that in relationships that last a long time, trust can be broken and rebuilt more than once. Trust is an organic process that evolves naturally over time.

93

How to End War

What I have come to understand is that I can't directly stop any of the many wars that are being fought around the world. But if I can wake up to the war inside me, if I can heal that inner violence, then I can bring an end to fighting. This happens as I wake up to the nature of my suffering, the causes and conditions of my life, and begin to doing things differently.

94

Plunging into Life

The aim of Zen practice is not to escape or transcend life's discomfort. Zen practice is about plunging into the mystery of daily life just as it is. Waking up involves touching my suffering, getting to know it intimately, and also touching my joy, my humor, and my love for others. An active meditation practice—one that acknowledges that all daily life activities are extensions of silent sitting—helps me to stop attempting to distract myself with activity, with noise and busyness, so that I can finally come into full contact with life.

95

War Is Not Inevitable

It is my firm conviction and clear understanding that while conflict is inevitable, the degeneration of conflict into slaughter, mayhem, and the abandonment of truth is not. War is not the result of human nature but of our unhealed, unaddressed suffering, which propels us to large-scale, industrialized killing. Killing at that level is the result of a fear-based worldview that drives us to seek safety by attempting the impossible: to control everything and everyone around us. Healing and transformation from this deadly and ever-tightening spiral is possible. We can live differently. War and suffering can be transformed. It is up us. Those of us who have begun to awaken to the true nature of violence—and the true nature of peace—can demonstrate, through the fabric of our lives, that there is a solution.

96

Alone But Not Isolated

I can feel very alone on this journey because it is in fact a journey that only I can take. But I don't have to take this journey in isolation. Telling our stories, sharing them, can lead to the creation of community, a loving community committed to living life differently. This community of like-minded people can then assist, help, support, and encourage each other in this process of waking up. Let us support each other—with our sadness, with our loss, with our despair—as two can carry it better than one. As you suffer, I suffer; as you heal, I heal. It is through this process that we begin to experience joy, the result of waking up and learning to live harmoniously with the whole self.

97

On Guilt

'Ve come to see guilt as a useful feeling, not to be confused with shame. Guilt tells me that I've done something that might not be alright. Shame tells me that fundamentally I'm not alright. I'm a soldier who fought in war. I took life. In facing that reality over time, I have learned to separate my guilt from my shame. I have also learned that the more I attempt not to feel guilt, the tighter that feeling holds me.

It took time and guidance to distinguish my guilt from my shame. When it comes to what I did in war, there is nothing I can ever do to change what happened. But I can learn to live differently now. I can take responsibility and dedicate my life to waking up to the war inside me, to share the message that violence is never a solution. Even when it seems like a solution, violence only gets more violence. Anger only gets more anger. War only gets more war.

I experience guilt about having abandoned my son for five years when he was a child. But that guilt is mine to deal with. I have to be careful not to let my guilt get in the way of being present in his life today. I can acknowledge my feelings without turning guilt or shame into a barrier.

98

Notice Any Feelings
of Superiority

To do the work of peace, to live the spiritual reality of life, I have no choice but to acknowledge that at whatever the level—individual, family, community, or nation—policies enacted from a perceived position of superiority will be exploitive, abusive, and dangerous. So I must look at where these seeds of superiority are in my life, see how they manifest themselves, and make a commitment not to turn away from this.

99

Transcend Cause and Effect

"There is a state of mind that surpasses cause and effect, a state other than the one in which we seek to gain 'that' by doing 'this.' It is a *samadhi* [meditative awareness] in which each instant is whole as it stands, in its totality. Each instant is reflected perfectly.

It is wonderful and necessary to throw one's energies into living in such a way as to plant, and thereby as to reap, the seeds of wholesome action within this limited world. Still, living a life solely based on the law of cause and effect—in the anticipation of future or immediate results—you will, without fail, come up against a barrier and feel despair.

By meeting what you are faced with right now, though, in this very instant, completely without judgment or evaluation, you can transcend by far all question of cause and effect."

—**Soko Morinaga**, *Novice to Master*

100

The Universality of Suffering

'Ve learned a great deal about myself and about the human condition on pilgrimage. I've witnessed the universality of suffering, how we all share the same essential problems, and the devastating and long-lasting effects of violence and war. What leads me to continue my practice is the most profound sense of responsibility not to let any of the lives that have been lost in any war be wasted. Those lives have been sacrificed to help us to wake up to the senselessness of war. War is not something that happens externally to us. In my understanding and in my experience, it is a collective expression of individual suffering. If we want war to stop, then we must wake up.

101

The Practice of
Saying Goodbye

When I was soldier in Vietnam, I stopped wanting to learn anything about the other soldiers, beyond what was printed on their name tag. If you came to my unit, I didn't want to get to know too much about you because you could die tomorrow. It seemed better just to stay distant and not to have to care or to feel.

Today, when our Zen community comes together for retreats, I make a point of paying special attention to how we say hello and goodbye to each other, approaching these two transition points as forms of practice. At the beginning of a retreat, we greet each other in the zendo, where we do a round of brief introductions. At the end of the retreat, we come back together in the zendo for a round of goodbyes, where participants are invited to restate their names and share whatever feelings or reflections feel necessary as part of saying goodbye.

We approach our goodbyes with careful attention, noticing the feelings that arise as we acknowledge the reality that we might not ever see each other again. Most of us are conditioned to avoid saying goodbye in a conscious way. We avoid acknowledging the loss of each other's presence and the uncertainty surrounding the future.

I have discovered over the years that when I say hello in a conscious way, an intimate connection is established. To keep this intimate connection alive in me, it is important to say goodbye with attention and awareness. When saying goodbye, I acknowledge a certain sense of loss that must be grieved. If I don't acknowledge this loss, at some point I will be confronted with a loss that I can't avoid, and the experience will be so much more challenging than it need be. At that point, all of the losses that I have avoided, and all of the grief connected with those losses, will come rushing to the surface. So my practice is to pay attention to each goodbye, allowing myself to be touched by the sorrow of that loss—which also makes me more available for the joy of hello.

102

Move beyond Thinking

My experience has shown me that waking up, that healing, is not a process of the intellect. It is not something that I can undertake with my thinking. There is no book to read, not even this one. I must thrust myself fully into life. I must look deeply into my nature and awaken to the fabric of how I have been conditioned to view the world, and into my own pain, so that I can begin to uncover and explore the nature of my experience.

103

Becoming Vulnerable

There isn't any healing without vulnerability. We must be open to the reality of ourselves and not hide from anything. The way to discover the nature of our suffering is to step directly into life. Challenging ourselves, compassionately, at every turn, really putting ourselves out there, being willing to make mistakes. That's where we learn about suffering and the way out of suffering.

104

Taking Responsibility
for Our Pain

There is a lot of projection that tends to go on when we suffer. We think that people or things outside ourselves are the causes of our suffering or could be the source of its relief. Our mind tells us if we eliminate the perceived source of the suffering, then it will be gone for good.

In war this way of thinking is encouraged and manifests in violence. Once embarking on this path, we become trapped in it; the violence controls us, creating a vicious circle that continues unchecked until we stop it by taking responsibility for our pain—by finding the courage to feel it, to enter into it, and not just to pass it on. If I don't look deeply into the nature of suffering, war continues.

105

The Zazen Person

"The merit of zazen [sitting meditation] appears within all aspects of the life of the zazen person. One should live to revere zazen as a most venerable buddha, being watched over by zazen and led by zazen. Zazen is not only when we sit on a zafu [cushion].

For a dedicated practitioner, there should be no gap between outward appearance and reality. Yet religionists often pretend to be holy persons in front of their believers. Eventually a gap arises between actuality and outward appearance. I believe that if even a slight gap arises, one cannot be a person of living religion.

This is especially important for a person who practices zazen as the self that is only the self. To practice zazen is to practice the reality of the self. If reality and outside appearances are different, the person's practice is no good at all. We should strictly live out the reality of the self."

—**Kosho Uchiyama**, *The Wholehearted Way*

106

Peace Is Not the Absence of Conflict

T hough my understanding of peace continues to grow and change, I do know that peace is not the absence of conflict; it's the absence of violence within conflict. To settle conflicts requires that we touch aggression, touch anger, touch the energy of violence, but that we do not surrender to these qualities within us. We can and must learn how to be in disagreement with each other. Conflict will exist; what matters is how we address it.

107

You Can Do This

You can do this. You can face your own sorrow, your own wounds. You can stop wanting some other life, some other past, some other reality. You can stop fighting against the truth of yourself and, breathing in and breathing out, open to your own experience. You can just feel whatever is there, exploring it, until you also discover the liberation that comes with stopping the struggle and becoming fully present in your own life. This is the real path to peace and freedom. In doing this for yourself, our whole world will benefit.

108

There Is Only Practice

n the end there is only practice. Everything, all the time, is meditation. Even our confusion, our fear, and our deep sadness are all points of practice. We only get lost if we are seeking some particular outcome or think that we ought to feel a certain way as a result of meditation practice. If I'm living a life rooted in meditation, I am invited to touch, to embrace the nature of my suffering without judging it.

We cannot think ourselves into a new way of living, we have to live ourselves into a new way of thinking. Pay attention to everything, to the smallest particle. It is in attending to the smallest particle that we discover the largest space, the fullness of a life thoroughly lived.

Bibliography

Cleary, Thomas (trans.). *Zen Lessons: The Art of Leadership.* Shambhala Publications, 2004.

Dogen, Eihei, Kosho Uchiyama (trans.), and Shohaku Okumura (trans.). *The Wholehearted Way.* Tuttle Publishing, 1997.

Easwaran, Eknath (trans.). *The Dhammapada.* Nilgiri Press, 2007.

Low, Albert. *The Iron Cow of Zen.* Tuttle Publishing, 1990.

Katigiri, Dainin. *Each Moment Is the Universe: Zen and the Way of Being Time.* Shambhala Publications, 2008.

Maezumi, Taizan and Bernie Glassman. *On Zen Practice: Body, Breath, and Mind.* Wisdom Publications, 2002.

Maezumi, Taizan and Wendy Egyoku Nakao. *Appreciate Your Life: The Essence of Zen Practice.* Shambhala Publications, 2002.

Morinaga, Soko and Belenda Attaway Yamakawa (trans.). *Novice to Master: An Ongoing Lesson in the Extent of My Own Stupidity.* Wisdom Publications, 2002.

Pine, Red (trans.). *The Zen Teachings of Bodhidharma.* North Point Press, 1989.

Thomas, Claude Anshin. *At Hell's Gate: A Soldier's Journey from War to Peace.* Shambhala Publications, 2004.

Uchiyama, Kosho. *Opening the Hand of Thought: The Foundations of Zen Practice.* Wisdom Publications, 2004.

Alphabetical Index of Titles

228

229

Acknowledgments

I am especially grateful for the engagement of those who have asked me questions during public talks and retreats. Your questions gave rise to the teachings presented in this book. Special thanks also to members of the Zaltho Zen Community in Italy, Germany, Chile, Colombia, and the United States for their contributions.

Thanks also to:

Eden MyoShin Steinberg, for stewarding me through the process of collecting, organizing, and editing the material that makes up this book—also for being hilariously funny and cooking good vegetarian chili.

Wiebke KenShin Beckmann-Andersen, for her editorial and proofreading help and for coordinating the diverse elements of bringing this book project to life.

Hilary Moreno, for her beautiful cover design and paw prints.

Marion GenRai Lukas, for her careful reading of the manuscript.

Carra Simpson, for her expertise, care, and support navigating the self-publishing process.

The Zaltho Foundation board of directors and advisors, for their ongoing commitment and support.

About the Author

Claude AnShin Thomas is a Zen Buddhist monk and the author of the book *At Hell's Gate: A Soldier's Journey from War to Peace.* At the age of 17 he enlisted in the US Army and served in the Vietnam War as a helicopter crew chief. Since that time, he has been working to heal the wounds of war—emotionally, mentally, and spiritually.

Ordained in Auschwitz in 1994 by Bernie Tetsugen Glassman, he walked on pilgrimage from Auschwitz to Vietnam, begging for alms along the way in the ancient Buddhist tradition of *takuhatsu.* He has walked several other pilgrimages since then in the United States and Europe.

Claude AnShin is the guiding teacher at the Magnolia Zen Center in Mary Esther, Florida, and the founder of the Zaltho Foundation, a nonprofit organization that promotes meditation and nonviolence. Claude AnShin teaches frequently in the United States, Europe, and South America. For more information, visit **www.zaltho.org** or email **info@zaltho.org**.

Also Available

At Hell's Gate: A Soldier's Journey from War to Peace

In this raw and moving memoir, Thomas describes his service in Vietnam, his subsequent emotional collapse, and his remarkable journey toward healing. "Everyone has their Vietnam," Thomas writes. "Everyone has their own experience of violence, calamity, or trauma." This book offers timeless teachings  on how we can all find healing, with practical guidance on how mindful awareness and compassion can transform our lives.

"Claude Anshin Thomas has been an inspiration to me. Our world urgently needs to listen to him tell of his life in war and then in peace."
—**Maxine Hong Kingston, author of** *The Woman Warrior*

"Written with relentless courage and utter compassion, this account of violence and transformation is one of the most amazing and wonderful stories I've ever read."
—**Michael Herr, Vietnam War correspondent and author of** *Dispatches*

Stay Connected with the Zaltho Zen Community

Join Our E-Mail List

Find out about retreats and other events, and get the latest news about the work of Claude AnShin Thomas and the Zaltho Foundation. Visit www.zaltho.org to sign up.

Subscribe to Our Podcast

The Zaltho Live podcast presents dharma talks and dialogues with Zen monk Claude AnShin Thomas exploring how Buddhist teachings and meditation practice can be brought to bear in all aspects of our lives. Now available on Apple iTunes, Spotify, Stitcher, and at www.zaltho.org.

Follow Us on Facebook

Follow the Zaltho Foundation Facebook page to learn about new audio and video teachings from Claude AnShin Thomas as they become available; enjoy short, inspirational teachings; and stay up-to-date on community news and events.

Made in the USA
Middletown, DE
25 April 2023